ANIMAL SAFARI

Wombats

by Margo Gates

BELLWETHER MEDIA • MINNEAPOLIS, MN

Note to Librarians, Teachers, and Parents:

Blastoff! Readers are carefully developed by literacy experts and combine standards-based content with developmentally appropriate text.

Level 1 provides the most support through repetition of high-frequency words, light text, predictable sentence patterns, and strong visual support.

Level 2 offers early readers a bit more challenge through varied simple sentences, increased text load, and less repetition of high-frequency words.

Level 3 advances early-fluent readers toward fluency through increased text and concept load, less reliance on visuals, longer sentences, and more literary language.

Level 4 builds reading stamina by providing more text per page, increased use of punctuation, greater variation in sentence patterns, and increasingly challenging vocabulary.

Level 5 encourages children to move from "learning to read" to "reading to learn" by providing even more text, varied writing styles, and less familiar topics.

Whichever book is right for your reader, Blastoff! Readers are the perfect books to build confidence and encourage a love of reading that will last a lifetime!

This edition first published in 2014 by Bellwether Media, Inc.

No part of this publication may be reproduced in whole or in part without written permission of the publisher. For information regarding permission, write to Bellwether Media, Inc., Attention: Permissions Department, 5357 Penn Avenue South, Minneapolis, MN 55419.

Library of Congress Cataloging-in-Publication Data

Gates, Margo.
  Wombats / by Margo Gates.
    p. cm. – (Blastoff! readers. Animal safari)
  Summary: "Developed by literacy experts for students in kindergarten through grade three, this book introduces wombats to young readers through leveled text and related photos"– Provided by publisher.
  Audience: K to grade 3.
  Includes bibliographical references and index.
  ISBN 978-1-60014-917-7 (hardcover : alk. paper)
  1. Wombats–Juvenile literature. I. Title.
  QL737.M39G38 2014
  599.2'4–dc23
                                                                      2013000891

Contents

What Are Wombats?

Wombats are **marsupials**. They have round bodies and short legs.

Females have **pouches** on their bellies. The pouches keep **joeys** warm.

A joey climbs into its mother's pouch after birth. Soon it grows too big for the pouch.

Burrows

Wombats live in forests and dry grasslands. They rest in **burrows** during the day.

burrow

Strong legs and wide feet help them dig burrows.

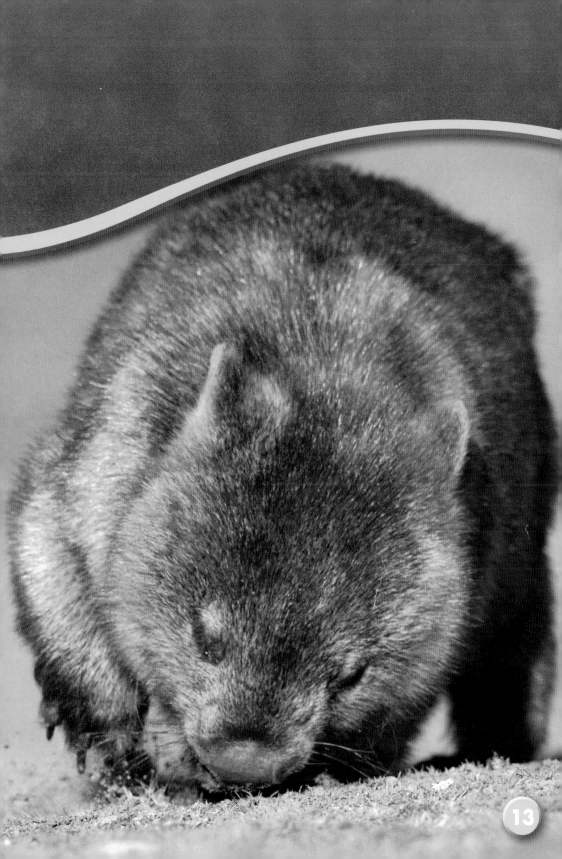

Eating

Wombats **graze** when the sun goes down. They eat grasses, **roots**, and tree bark.

They **gnaw** on their food. This keeps their sharp teeth short.

Escaping Danger

Wombats run from dingoes, foxes, and other **predators**.

They dive into their burrows. Then they block the tunnels with their bodies!

Glossary

burrows—holes or tunnels that some animals dig in the ground

gnaw—to bite or chew on something to wear it down

graze—to eat grasses and other plants

joeys—baby marsupials

marsupials—animals that carry their young in a pouch attached to the belly

pouches—pockets of skin on the bellies of female marsupials

predators—animals that hunt other animals for food

roots—the parts of plants that grow into the ground

To Learn More

AT THE LIBRARY
Arnold, Caroline. *A Wombat's World*.
Minneapolis, Minn.: Picture Window Books,
2008.

Kras, Sara Louise. *Wombats*. Mankato, Minn.:
Capstone Press, 2010.

Shields, Carol Diggory. *Wombat Walkabout*.
New York, N.Y.: Dutton Children's Books,
2009.

ON THE WEB
Learning more about
wombats is as easy as 1, 2, 3.

1. Go to www.factsurfer.com.

2. Enter "wombats" into the search box.

3. Click the "Surf" button and you will see a
   list of related Web sites.

With factsurfer.com, finding more information
is just a click away.

Index

The images in this book are reproduced through the courtesy of: Juan Martinez, front cover, p. 5; Minden Pictures/ Masterfile, p. 7; Andrew Forsyth/ FLPA/ Age Fotostock, p. 9; NHPA/ SuperStock, p. 11; Subbotina Anna, p. 11 (left); ODM, p. 11 (right); Andrew Forsyth/ FLPA, p. 13; Dave Watts/ Visuals Unlimited, Inc./ Getty Images, p. 15; Yellowj, p. 15 (left); Richard Griffin, p. 15 (middle); Jiri Haureljuk, p. 15 (right); Steffen & Alexandra Sailer/ Ardea, p. 17; Dave Watts/ Biosphoto, p. 19; SF photo, p. 19 (left); Ian Rentoul, p. 19 (right); Rob Walls/ Alamy, p. 21.